Hi there!

Every parent marvels at the way their children learn new things. From the first time they sit up to when they take their first steps and say their first words, each moment is magical and to be savoured.

I was told that reciting nursery rhymes and reading out loud from early on would help a baby's language development, so I was very excited to hear that Tumble Tots was bringing out a book on this topic. The rhymes here are great – you can use them to show children parts of their body and also to help them make word associations.

So, here it is... Ten Little Fingers, a compilation of beautifully illustrated body identification rhymes.

I can see my youngest and I acting out these rhymes over and over again and I am sure you and your children will enjoy them as much too!

Sally Gunnell

Ten Little Fingers

WHat's insiDe?

Look out for Wiggly woo popping up in this book!

Ten Little Fingers

Ten little fingers,

Ten little toes,

wiggle your **fingers** and **thumbs**

wiggle all your **toes**

Two little ears,

And one little nose.

hold your **ears** and wiggle

touch your **nose**

PARENTS' NOTES

Encourage children to recognise and name parts of their body. With younger children, sit down together, say the rhyme and help them point to each part. Older children can copy your actions.

5

Two little eyes for me to see,

point to your **eyes**

And one little mouth to eat my tea.

point to your **mouth** and pretend to eat

ROUND AND ROUND THE GARDEN

Round and round the garden,

Like a teddy bear,

One step, two steps,

Tickly under there!

Round and round the haystack,

Like a little mouse,

One step, two steps,

Right inside the house.

Point to it!
Can you find two brown mice?

9

CLaP YOUR HaNDs 1, 2, 3

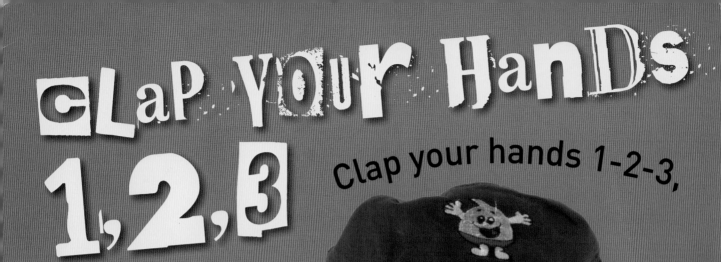

Clap your hands 1-2-3,

clap your **hands**

Pat your hands on your knees.

pat your **knees**

11

Wave them way up high in the sky,

wave your **hands** in the air

12

Clap clap hands, away they fly.

clap your **hands**

hold out your **arms,** then wiggle your **fingers**

13

1, 2, 3, 4, 5 once i caught a

1-2-3-4-5,

Once I caught a fish alive.

6-7-8-9-10,

Then I let him go again.

FiSH aLiNe

POint tO it!
Can you spot three
green frogs?

Why did you let him go?

Because he bit my finger so!

Which finger did he bite?

This little finger on my right.

i Have two eyes

I have two eyes to see,

I have two feet to run,

point to both **eyes**

tap your **feet**
on the ground quickly

16

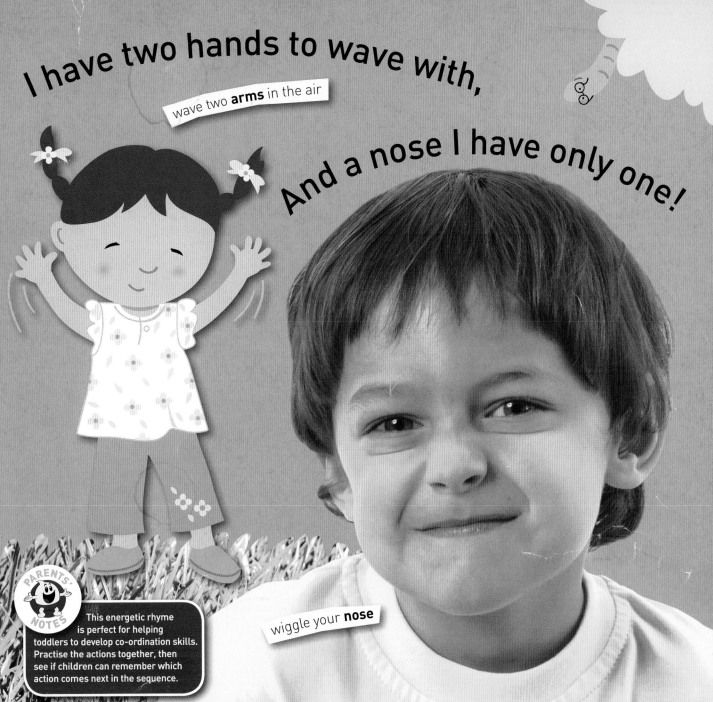

I have two hands to wave with,

wave two **arms** in the air

And a nose I have only one!

wiggle your **nose**

17

i HaVe twO ears

I have two ears to hear with,
One mouth to say 'Good day'.

Good day!

hold your **ears** and wiggle them

wiggle your **tongue**

PARENTS' NOTES
Why not read this rhyme to children and look at the pictures together first? What are ears for? What is your mouth for? What is the girl saying? Then practise the actions and shout out 'Good day'!

18

I have two cheeks for you to pinch,

gently pinch your **cheeks**

And then I run away!

run on the spot

19

Butterfly

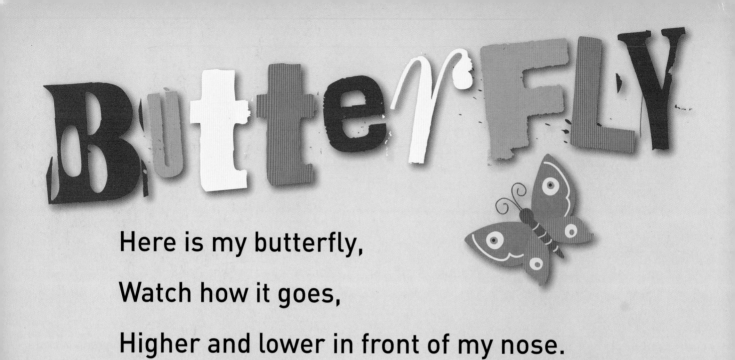

Here is my butterfly,

Watch how it goes,

Higher and lower in front of my nose.

Point to it!
How many butterflies
can you see?

It started out tiny,

And then grew and grew,

It fluttered about, then off it flew.

21

Let's wiggle

Wiggle your fingers in the air,

stretch your **arms** and wiggle your **fingers**

PARENTS' NOTES

Learn about different parts of your hand. With younger children, sit down together and help them with the actions. Encourage older children to name each part as they act out the rhyme.

Wiggle them here and wiggle them there.

wiggle your **fingers** from side to side

23

Fingers and thumbs,

Nails and palms,

show your **fingers**, then **thumbs**

rub your **nails** together, then your **palms**

24

You'll find your hands at the end of your arms.

roll out your **arms**,
then open your **hands**

25

Teddy Bear

Teddy Bear, Teddy Bear dance on your toes,

Teddy Bear, Teddy Bear touch your nose,

Teddy Bear, Teddy Bear pat your head,

Teddy Bear, Teddy Bear go off to bed,

Teddy Bear, Teddy Bear wake up now,

Teddy Bear, Teddy Bear make your bow.

POint to it!

Can you find the teddy bear touching its nose?

27

i can

I can stretch my arms up high,

stretch your **arms** above your **head**

I can touch the ground,

bend down and touch the floor

I can shake my head about,

gently shake your **head**

And never make a sound.

place your **finger**
to your **lips**

29

I can jump and dance and clap,

There's so much I can do.

jump, wiggle and clap

Yes, I can sing my 'I can' songs,

point to yourself

30

And you can sing them too!

point to someone else

31